MAST YEARS: POEMS

MAST YEARS: POEMS

GUY CRAIG

THOUGHTS ON THE GOOD LIFE PRESS
Oregon, USA

MAST YEARS: POEMS

Published by

THOUGHTS ON THE GOOD LIFE PRESS

Portland, Oregon

www.ThoughtsOnTheGoodLife.com

© Copyright 2022 by GUY CRAIG

Poetry

Written by GUY CRAIG

Artwork by GUY CRAIG

Cover Art by SARAH CRAIG

First Edition

For inquires, write to the author, with the subject line "Inquires," at the email address below.

Hello@ThoughtsOnTheGoodLife.com

Visit - GuyCraigPoetry.com

This book is a work of fiction. Names, characters, places, and incidents either are the product of the author's imagination or are used fictitiously, and any resemblance to actual persons, living or dead, events, organizations, or locales is entirely coincidental.

ISBN: 978-1-7334968-5-8

*For Sarah, Kenneth, and the gifts granted
in the Mast Years we entertain.*

SECTION I: HOME

Mast Years   *4*
Photo Albums   *5*
Small Town   *6*
Herb Garden   *7*
Stories of Home   *8*
Home Projects   *9*
Private Walks   *10*
Paintings of Home   *11*
Cutting Boards   *12*
Wind   *13*
Water   *14*
Fire   *15*
Earth   *16*

SECTION II: TIME

Booms and Busts 21
Dinner Table 22
Landscaping 23
Trails 24
Sanctuary 25
Clothing Lines 26
Keep Enough 27
Preserving 28
Safely Rely Upon 29
Rain Gauges 30
Hummingbirds 31
Garden Flowers 32
The Lightest View 33
Pets 34
Softened Sounds 35
Decks, Porches, and Pavillions 36
Flower Arrangements 37
Game Rooms 38
Spirit Cabinet 39
Bookshelves 40
Seasons Change 41
Other Worlds Have I 43
Slow Time 47
Limited Tomorrows 48

SECTION III: IDEAS

Cataloged 51
Hold You 52
Creeks at Home 53
Generous Hosts 54
Memories to Forget 55
Arts and Crafts 56
Music 57
Local Trips 58
Gifting 59
Retired Neighbors 60
Add Time 61
Local Works 62
Open Doors and Windows 63

Notes 65
Acknowledgments 66

MAST YEARS: POEMS

SECTION I
HOME

*My sight. In those moments, home
In my mind was finally owned.*

Uniform days until the Mast Years
Return to remind—life is change

—

Mast Years

Some seasons, the trees turn out
Overabundance together. The years are variable.
Mast Years conspicuously cap the ground
With hearty spheres of crunching sound
As nuts as seeds. The notes
Play percussion in songs sung steadily
In a rhythm that reveals life
In its yields. The Mast Years
Rarely live back-to-back. Curiously, most often
The wheel of predator and prey
Turn on temperate and dry springs
That boast the most tree blooms.
The right breezes before open flowers
Purpose the pollen to a fortune
Expanded as victual, on the earth,
Where too much, too quickly, spoils
For no lack of hunger. Full
Forests are foretold in the seeds
Nature has farmed and fertilized. After
All has been gleaned, the predators
Become the prey. The wheel turns.
The expansive and contractive world remembers
Uniform days until the Mast Years
Return to remind—life is change.

Photo Albums

Today, I found all the forgotten
Photos. They were buried in boxes
With books deep in the study.
With just a little more leisure,
They will become a selected sight.
Each album will mark an era.
All the family, friends, and company
Will live on in laughs shared
Together. The good years will outnumber
The bad. I might only see
The unhappy moments in the background.
I look forward to the forgotten
Visitors who I held the highest
Moments with. I might even remember
An old story or two sealed
In the dried film of joy
And mirth we once all entertained.
I will make some more photos
On the special days I design
The albums. Maybe they will frame
How I fill the empty spaces.

Small Town

I am from a small town
Where big dreams are the best
Ones worth having. There is just
Enough room to believe you can
Accomplish whatever you set your aims
To achieving. My small town arose
From light, settled-saltwater and heavy, saturated sandstone
So recently that the only diamonds
From the land will be made
In the far future from today's
Coal. The trees in the fog
Feed the soil that gives life
To everything grown. Purpose takes care
Of the people, the water gives
Them life, the land gives them
A home. The world may want
To be only one prominent city-state—
Most people from small towns hope
For better prosperity where they are
Living and to be left alone.

Herb Garden

If woodland spirits can be found
In the wild places of imagination,
Maybe they can visit the constructed
Plots of contained proximity. Enriched
Spaces designed to flavor the favored
Foods enjoyed during my youth. Magical
Meals are now rare, reasoned recipes.
The family, who remain, are distant.
I know they remember the rituals
We called family get-togethers, the foods
Prepared, and the seasonings once shared.

Stories of Home

Stories sow into you. The people
With a shared vision of home
As a place of purpose that exists
Even after the land is gone.
For the sake of the children
The exiled seek new dawns. Away
From the long line of ancestors
From one place, with one heart,
The new land somehow seems less
Consequential. The water and the earth
Of the new land feels different
From old grounds that helped grow
The family. The stories of home
Are maps to places others own.
When I remember how I travel
Each day past cherished memories adapted
To fit my newfound understanding,
I try to leave more room
In my belief for better days
Ahead. Abundant days may again arrive
Brightening prospects to gather the gains
I can lightly and colorfully enjoy
Communally. The best stories graft past
Ways to celebrate what is cyclical
In new lands as they unfold.

Home Projects

The other day, you were working
Like you never retired. Your energy
Returned after its dormancy. It awakened
Before our eyes, and we watched
With wonder at what you accomplished.
Home projects fell before your saw.
The toothed-scything through the thick trees
Was thunderous. The reverberations of tasks
Completed with no breaks in between
Reminded us of when lunch was
Always a dirty word. Taking breaks
And asking questions while you worked—
Penalized the gift of gratuitous production.

Private Walks

Private wilderness walks are quietly enjoyed
Best by people who are wary
Of judgements. They know the walks
Are exceedingly energizing in natural proportion
To fewer people along the paths.
They intuitively appreciate and ingeniously understand
That the lives of wise wanders
Measure success by how much privacy
Is enjoyed each day. I prosper
Most in my life when observant
Nature is my destination. Those times
In my heart, when I have
Given thanks for all the blessings
The forest has set to share
In the restful arches of air
As the earth's sturdy palatial pines.
Just the other day, I felt
Contentment with the world around me.
I had never felt so favored.
I watched the westerly-birds fly freely
Away with my cares. I listened
To the sounds of their wings,
And I imagined I understood why
Angels fly as light in dark
Places. I walked and I wandered.

Paintings of Home

My favorite painting of home shows
The house in spring from the south.
The painter stood in the tall,
Healthy, and undergrazed grass. Boots covered
With pollen and numerous new seeds
From a field full of fortune
For the next season's hungry gain—
The hope for tomorrow. The images
Display peace with just the perfect
Impression of clarity. Like my memories,
A soft layered filter enhances missing
Details I fill in with joyful
Composites gleaned through select sounds, scents,
And textures. The oil painting preserves
What I often see myself becoming
In the picture where I wasn't
Brushed. I am free to move
With my family who I see
Inside the intricate frame. I hope
My present home someday arrives to
Bespeak for family whose love repeats.

Cutting Boards

In my youth, the Oregon Coast
Wasn't merely the majestic, soundly sea.
Most lived near bays and rivers.
Everyone had a favorite fragrant tree
Species. Lumber flowed from sturdy saw
Mills. Massive wood chip piles climbed
As high as ancient old-growth timber.
Hills of money, memorably ocean bound
As wood chips, were valued to
Paper ideas in an unwrapped world.
Ink's mate journeyed over the ocean's
And far land's rough, winding paths.
Myrtlewood was in every kitchen. Cutting
Boards were a metaphor for harvests
Made deep in the damp forests.
Corporate capital and careful cutters fought
Both each other and private elements.
The timber in the tracks deeply
Held their hopeful and shared imagination.
Many believed in an inexhaustible harvest.
Size and scale were often confused
For constant renewal. Now—cutting boards,
Framed with wood from the forests,
Hold hands with ancestors who remain.

Wind

All air awaits within atmospheric invitations.
Gentle winds fan the world. Helpful
Fans fill homes with ample opportunities
To enjoy soft, managed, mechanical breezes
When open windows and doors need
to stay closed to better brace
For closed moments. The open moon-winds
Sometimes gust most brightly when full
Visions give a sense of purpose.
Century storms arrive as an aberration
With local terrain. Century storms predict
Change on a time scale saturated
With near misses and meandering consistency.
Gentle breezes often belie the gusty
Return of landscapes barren and broken
In a world striving to withstand
What the weather brings. The land
Will heal again in variable intervals,
With often steady and aching work
By the wind-touched who steadily remain
Able to welcome the wind's ways.

Water

Some water is to be welcomed.
Water returned to the soil sailed.
Some say storing water stills sadness.
Homes are most natural when nestled
Between puddles, pools, and ponds. Some
Say waves of emotional power precipitate
People's peaceful purposes. The other day,
Waves of rain washed away salt-laden
Tears. Far from the formidable ocean,
I crested with the wandering water
To other homes I have known.
I have waited for replenishing returns
To water tables of guiltless joy
And simple meaning I once knew
Before the drought of prolonged dullness.
On the tide, for a moment,
My youthful spirit followed the river
With deep appreciation and affectionate awe
For loved ones who moved past
My sight. In those moments, home
In my mind was finally owned.

Fire

The heat from the fire warms
More than my body. The light
Focuses my attention on the flame.
I peer patiently with an ignited
Understanding that my energy for answers
Will be depleted before my questions.
I keep fire in my sight,
Knowing that even brief, charcoal-spent moments
Still have energy to bring light.

Earth

A little earth contained isn't always
Going to make you feel grounded.
It might help. When you plant
Seeds in the soil, the future
Seems more bountiful. The more plants
Cleaning the air and abstracting interior
Design elements grown from the earth
Can artfully affect a home's climate.
When it is clean of chemicals,
The closer it is to nature.
You might find yourself in all
The cozy corners of the space
You love best. With any luck,
The sheltered land you live in
Helps you with your careful choices.
Every gardener understands—nourish to grow.

Blame before all else. Reason loses
Against hate. Hidden truths unburried openly

—

You love best. With any luck,
The sheltered land you live in

—

SECTION II
TIME

*Through the tests of time. Extremes
Of nature tell of the need*

Booms and Busts

Booms and busts are the reason
Humans first recorded laws and history.
The Big Bang theory of cosmology
Shares a truth with Mast Years.
Big wins and wealth received unexpectedly
Are welcomed times that can be
Short-lived and not always equally shared,
Which can make others long darkly
For what is another's good fortune.
History records the rise and fall
Of civilizations, and only the people
Born to live in the middle
Seem capable of measuring the extremes
Of behavior and belief. The unhealthy
Blame before all else. Reason loses
Against hate. Hidden truths unburied openly
Enlightens. Effortful objectivism cannot be replaced.

Dinner Table

When my son was in kindergarten,
He sometimes loved to sit calmly
At our small dining room table.
At those special times, I understood
How sitting together at eye level
Elevates the ones before us. He
Became my vision of his future.
I saw his humanity. I marveled.
I saw our time together was more
Than posture, patience, and protocols. Etiquette
Expanded time to see each other.
Like other families, we share time
Together to teach each other how
We might travel when we're apart.
Our table has plenty of room
For us now and for after
We complete our other outside obligations.
When the dinner table is empty,
I still see him before me.

Landscaping

Some land was shaped by humans
Some say to better endure beyond
The constraints of long, natural cycles.
After deep mourning, did some begin
To understand relationships have a shape?
From the tender of Mast Years,
How long did prey peacefully feed
On the abundant crop of nuts?
How long until predators eventually outnumbered
The prey? When a Mast Year
Returned, did someone loudly yell: "no
More hungry winters?" Did anyone listen?
Was the first honorary title called:
"The King's Gardener?" Was his garden
The reason for the first perimeter?
Some land was shaped by humans.
Some say landscapes sow all successions.

Trails

Out the door, the trails lead
To coastal mountains and open-aired spaces,
Where anything might move more freely.
Beautiful flowers—no matter how sparsely
Grown—may seed more fragrant settings.
Some blooms await the right season.
Some seasons arrive to welcomed exuberance.
Each year, I hope to travel
On trails that change direction outside
My understanding. I hope to learn
The great truths that seem happy
To live closest to the land.

Sanctuary

Most people stay where they are
Their whole lives. It is natural
To bond where one is grown.
Like branches bending to the light,
We are shaped by our needs
To adapt to our environment. Outside
Our comfort zone, we may stretch
Our capacities beyond any reasonable limits.
Healing is a long, hellish hope
That tightly binds. Over time, mistakes
Set us back and carefully craft
The ways we build a sanctuary
In our minds. Some people craft
A place filled with the senses
Of home. Some peace is near
The favored scents of loved trees
Arranged neatly. A small fountain holds
The rocks and charms of memories
Better contained than forgotten. Private settings
Of cherished comfort honor the order
That brings peace with what's known.

Clothing Lines

The sun stiffly dries the sundries
On the clothing lines this afternoon.
Just the right amount of heat
Holds the clothes and towels together
In the weathered ways I remember
From times before the dryer worked
Fine and responsibilities weren't for me.
I like heavily starched towels set
Like camp tents in the heat
Of the day as a creator
Of shade. Somehow my clothes wear
More substantially. In my youth, I
Sometimes mistook the many repetitive, stable
Chores as family sternness when fastidiousness
Naturally reflected the years of hardiness
And want. All I often see
Is plenty. I have not been
Keeping the time. I do not
Know all the family histories informing
The caution, economy, and the fear
That was kept in the dark,
Away from me in my youth.
I was the child who was
Given the chance to finally live
As the past generations had never
Dreamed was possible without more light.

Keep Enough

I could never keep enough freedom.
As a child, I was both
Poor and wealthy. I always had
Two loving parents, one family land,
And a brother to play pretend
With that we would never need

To work to make a living
Or worry about helping with chores.
I had pleasure for purpose, memories
As momentary as a light morning
Mist. I entertained my entitlement completely
Unaware that I was taking without

Giving. Pain and loneliness takes away
From the wealth we don't appreciate.
With indulgence, I spread the spaces
Of emptiness I left for others.
I was poorer with every acquisition.
License isn't freedom. Restraint isn't chains.

Preserving

Preserving the harvest to last longer
Comes from the natural and perennial
Understanding that some goods are limited.
Like the animals who store food
For the winter, all people sense
How quickly hunger returns. Abundance
May produce extra yearly food helpings
That are dry enough to last
Longer than what is eaten wet
Daily. The old fruit turns stronger.
One spoil leads to other questions
Of what else might bring surprises.
The wine is drunk to preserve
Water. The herd is to save
Chase. The new plantings still haste.

Safely Rely Upon

There are some days you can
Safely rely upon. The wonderful memories
Given to people from happy seasons
Are for appreciation. Judgment and grace
Exist as an acknowledgment of eternal
Goods of both limited and unlimited
Meaning. The goods of fortune accompany
Moments for reflection and quiet awe
In the understanding that some purpose
Is luck and some luck is
Purpose. It is the sharing, protecting,
And preserving of private, real goods,
And public norms and rules agreed
Upon by citizens that protect against
The expedient and the secret actions
That malign the spirit of collaboration
Through the tests of time. Extremes
Of nature tell of the need
To rely upon tomes and talismans
That record the start of new
Cycles of old peaks and valleys.

Rain Gauges

In the rainy seasons, I like
To watch the rain gauge measure
The rate of the water replenishing
The soil. The dividend of rain
Is safe. My frequent walks past
The gauge offers me visible confirmation
That everything is within the normal
Range for the moment. Price books,
Like rain gauges, record the real
Bargains. Sales advertisements of great deals
Cannot honestly hide the right time
To buy or not sell. The deluge
Of extraordinary opportunities to understand relative
Value is worth the effort. Maneuvering
Past landslides, freshets, and fear wisely
Provides for prosperous and manageable advantages.

Hummingbirds

You always seem to favor hummingbirds
Over other wild animals. These birds
Seem to favor you more than
The rest of us. We watch
Out for the seemingly near misses
From the miniature but mighty creatures
Who frequent the back deck feeder.
Especially in the winter, their fierceness
Broadcasts as brightly as the male's
Colors. The sounds of their wings
Precisely prepares us steadily for messages
That some people say silently share
Loss. I suppose I understand why
You care for them so deeply.
Your losses were earlier than most.
Your struggles to synthesize arrived before
You had time to fully appreciate
All the gains you would know
As an adult. The consistent challenges
Often overshadowed the successes that occasioned
You to react in certain ways.
I now see that in between
All of the flights of fortitude,
You were constantly feeding the lives
Of the ones who loved home.

Garden Flowers

Is it luck to generously grow
In a place where needs are
Wrapped in the water? Fate arrives
Like a memory in reverse. Choice
Ebbs and flows with our perceptions
Of favored outcomes. The strongest flowers
Thrive through the revealed regular rhythms
By blooming with hopeful pastel harvests.
Beauty never stays too late. True
Gifts grown for goodness display light
Expressions of consolation when contentment ceases.
When the garden greys into memory,
The fresh flowers' scents and colors
Remain to remind of better days.

The Lightest View

The lightest view is the one
That allows for thoughts to trail
On the wind with the wait.
In the right settings, the seasons
Change the sounds that carry over
The ground. Natural feelings gradually gather
With the gains that give gratitude
In the same measure they give
Forgiveness. Deep feelings deliver the calmness
Sought by staying silent and still.

Pets

A little life around the house
Can add to the life within.
Paws pattering on morning-cooled floors predict
The following steps in the day's
Activities. Some sounds of movement set
The pace for pets' daily purposes.
Like anything in life, the number
Of pets one owns should correspond
To ability and resources. Moderation leads
Many people to understand that care
Takes energy and time. The joy
Of their unique personalities shared together
In marked memories is a measure
Of grateful gains and lamented, labored
Losses. The absense of long-lived listeners'
Pain is salved when securely settled
Next to the wistfully-welcomed fond friends
Remembered. The moments of wondrous wildness
Shared together must sometimes be enough.

Softened Sounds

Softened sounds are natural in nature.
Only in their long, uninvited absence
Do we begin to understand we
Are finely weaved from the wrapped-wilderness,
Togetherness is both choice and chance,
And every invited, quiet moment makes
Meaning in a noisy world. Soft
Settings are secured for serene seers
Of imagination and every genuine inquiry
Gifts the world more generous knowledge
For every well-intentioned person to own.

Decks, Porches, and Pavilions

Decks and porches are a home's
Pavilions. Nature is the play. All
The elements are a theatrical troop
Who only live to perform. Thespian
Talents reflect that the world performs
A sharing process of continuous absorption.

Flower Arrangements

I always love the arranged flowers
In the rooms. The arrangements shower
Our home with warmth and abundance.
I often carry their beauty to
Ugly places where pain colors sound.
I marvel that anyone can care
Enough about sharing the little things
In life—the extra energy required
In the garden to grow flowers,
Ferns, and other flora for vases
In the spaces that appear central
To a joyful and colorful existence.
Fragrant mornings lead to meaningful moments
Memorialized in my mission to help
You see how much you mean
To me and all who know
You. Know, when I arrange flowers,
Your love of beauty is sown.

Game Rooms

Game rooms illuminate the biggest parties.
They also festively brighten small family
Gatherings. There is a comforting confirmation
That in this sometimes-severe and serious
World, there is room to explore
Processes that play with fundamental rules
That hint at the nature of who
We really are, what is fair
Chance, and what is calculated choice.
A game room at its best
Is a museum of the memorialized,
Helpful, and enduring challenges of right
Over might. The perfect puzzles excite
The players' sense of personal cleverness.
The games are low stakes shows
Of skill. Games are a glimpse
Into the spirit of the players.
They are a convex mirror maze
That reflectively err from expectations in
Proportion to how well they delight
From without. Game rooms are tricksters'
Temples to surprise. The playful know
Only too well that some evoke
Intense emotion, yet not every win
Or loss gives reason to dwell.

Spirit Cabinet

Some people like to secure spirits
Next to their tonics. Bubbles in
Their drinks add to life's mixture
Of satisfying solutions that bring change
In a measured and consistent cycle.
Others like to know they can
Be ready to host company well
On unannounced visits. I like sharing
A few of my meaningful memories
With welcomed guests. Long-known friends remember
Better with a late-favored playful potion
From wilder and more westerly days.

Bookshelves

Every home I have ever seen
Has had a lovely empty corner
Where I imagine the space fully
Lined with books on a shelf.
All rooms can become a study.
Bookshelves provide a way to order
Values we have acquired and received
Over our lives. Sometimes books arrive
In batches. I have kept books
My grandfather read. His revered books
Were next to his study table
Along a shelf to his right.
They were always easy to find—
At eye level and within reach.
They are close to me now.
I have my own selection stored
And I know it was influenced
By his books that I read.
I clearly see their location together
On the bookshelf as a reminder
To add to my own curated
Collection while I have the inclination
And the ability to occasionally ponder
Some of the world's perennial problems.

Seasons Change

As an old parent, I was
Reminded that ten percent or more
Of listed lessons in grade school
Regularly revolve around the school calendar.
The holidays and seasons are steady
Topics to teach the young children
Who know nothing but that everything
Changes surprisingly quickly. As they grow,
Each day is a whole adventure.
Schools seem to understand the need
For children to receive something revisited
Each year. There is a comfort
In the ritual of celebrating days
Of special meaning that change slowly
As part of a long conversation
Society communicates with itself. It's natural
To understand and practice the best
That can be taught by learning
About the holidays that honor humanity.

I also know how honored holidays
And seasonal celebrations are understood changes
As the world's voices of views
Are added to the pages. Distance
Of feelings of people who lived
Long ago is hard to hear
And reconcile with our own time
And place. When my child contemplates
All the holidays and the seasons
I give thanks that we all
Have something left to still share
Together. I humbly pray each day,
That tomorrow may finally bring enlightenment
To find ways to thrive tenderly
With the seasons that wondrously remain.

Other Worlds Have I

I grew up in a mountain
Canyon next to a tidal river
And fields that grew from sandstone
That had been set and seasoned.
Home felt like fine ocean sand.
My emotions sometimes moved in sync
With the tides. On cloudless nights,
I watched the moon and images
Far above me and I absorbed
The words my mother would say
As she looked to the heavens:
"Other worlds have I." She believed
The church of her childhood taught
That idea. Though, we couldn't find
It in the Bible or other
Books that they shared. Incredible revelations
Such as this were not unique.

She told of aliens and ghosts.
As a child of the church,
She would attend the early services
With her grandparents, who lived in
A home with a flat roof.
One weekend, they went home early.
When they pulled up, she saw
A saucer-shaped ship (with three legs)
Populated with aliens she could witness
Moving past the windows. She whispered
With fear and surprise to her
Grandparents. They said that they saw
Nothing. She told me this story
Whenever I asked. She said it
Was the truth. She was not
Sure why they could not see
What was so clearly above them.

She once saw an unsettled apparition
In the old, rundown ranch house
She and my father moved into
And achingly remodeled after they married.
The ghost sometimes slammed a bedroom's
Door until she one day yelled:
"This is my home now. Leave!
We are staying. You must go."
That night, upon waking, she heard
A sound downstairs. As she stood
At the top of the stairs—
Below—she saw an old man
Dressed in a white suit staring
Observantly. The ghost was silent. Light
Flickered and he was gone. After
That night, doors did not slam,
And he was not seen again.

As an adult, I sometimes look
Up and down my mother's river,
Up to the stars on clear
Nights and down to the ground
Where deep-spirited, sailing moon shadows lightly
Play with the grasses and branches.
I see a physical world around
Me and I interpret spiritual worlds
That I sense. I cannot always
Easily share their connection with others.
It's that view of the world
That compels me to keep searching
For ways to see other's confirmations
In the delightful and delicate sights.

Slow Time

Always having instant access to technology
Has been a relative and expanding
Concern of society from the beginning
Of human existence. The trends increase
Through time with breaks and reversals
In the short term. Today is
One of those eras where changes
In technology are at an extreme
Pace. Technology can often open paths
Through life's quieter landscapes as terribly
As a tornado moves through towns.
Not every tendency to slow time
Limits chances of continuing to exist.
Sometimes we need to slow time
In the chaos to find ways
To become more resilient. All life
Needs to have moments of solitude
And rest. Sometimes our best solutions
Are found when we have space.

Limited Tomorrows

Some people are lost in leaner
Times. They hold on to each
Calorie uncarefully and every heavy meal
They eat is confirmation that abundance
Is still their good fortune. Times
Of need do not always arrive
When they are expected. Sometimes, colossal
Cycles begin of predator and prey
Just at the moment we telegraph
There will always be enough food
To provide for rich and happy
Lives. Get healthy while you can.
Mast Years are often achingly unpredictable.
Extra seeds and nuts may grow
Again, but they do so slowly.
Their abundance may produce for future
Generations. You only have limited tomorrows
To store unlimited goods against regrets.

SECTION III
IDEAS

*Hosts who celebrate sweet, long welcomes
The way I celebrate speedy goodbyes.*

Cataloged

I like to work backward in
Scale. All the world far away
Seems cataloged, while my countryside stays
Hidden. I have written a host
Of ideas on what is most
Meaningful. Proximity is my perennial preoccupation.
The books in my study share
Ways to navigate through abundant nature
Around me. I have many books
On plants that grow best nearby
My home. The plants are all
Pictured and recorded in the pages.
The fauna that feed on plants
And each other have names recorded
With special care and they are
Often pictured with the images illustrated
At home. I like to add
New entries as I find them,
This gives me a good reason
To deliberately go outside each day.
New life finds ways over old
Paths I have honored my way.

Hold You

If I could securely show you
All the people in the world
Who hold you dear, you'd believe
In miracles. You cannot clearly see
All of the varied well wishes
Sent your way throughout the day.
Your heart might not fully hear
All of the sounds of celebration
In each of your unrecognized achievements.
I think you would be tenderly
Amazed with the love the world
Has for you and its hope
To hold you in its health.
It might soften those challenging times
Before and memorably make them slightly
Less painful. You might even strengthen
More quickly as you lightly lift
Up others you observe in despair.
The world is a busy place.
Silence may not mean sanctions. Past
Good will shared leaves a trace.

Creeks at Home

In Coos River coastal canyons, creeks
Flow through iron-infused sandstone pressed together
From the sands of the once
Ocean floors. The water moving through
The canyons ebb and flow seasonally.
Springs are often the primary sources
Of water for the creeks. Rain
Does its part too. And I
Am one of the lucky ones
Who gets to see the cycles
Clear the meandering creeks past home.

Generous Hosts

Some places have the precise location
To let light shine most magnificently
With a warm comfort and ease
Through the good hosts of heart
And mind. When the hosts hone
Their energy and creativity with others
Magic happens. Something ethereal honors creation.
The world magnifies as a gentle
And friendly place. We purpose together
Outside the caves of our survival.
We venture forth in festive exuberance
With enjoyment that can neither be
Weighed nor partitioned. The hosts project
An expression of our better angels.
They honor the people in testament
Written in words invisible and endearing.
I always give a tender thanks
To all the glorious and generous
Hosts who celebrate sweet, long welcomes
The way I celebrate speedy goodbyes.

Memories to Forget

I rarely recall all the words
To a song or a poem.
Anything above a few stanzas disappears
To a place I imagine I
Store leisurely ideas for a later
Date to rediscover. I have techniques
To help when I imagine I
Must have a memorized line ready
For use. It often bothered me
To slowly learn that had I
A voice for verse, I might
Always need the words and notes
Before me. Now that I'm older,
I try understanding memory in reverse.
The more I write, the less
I have to remember. The best
Answers I discover while writing surprise
Me. I write memories to forget.

Arts and Crafts

I often elevate the analog arts
And crafts of my youth. Celebrated
Activities shared through the gifted generations
Allow me to feel the richness
Of life and offer me opportunities
To gratefully catch some unexpected glimpses
Of answers to archival questions asked
In reflective gazes from lost days.

Music

Music received right on time lifts
The spirit. A satisfying life often
Is rich with sound and rhythm
To enchantingly ease and soothe regrets
From the highest past joys lost
Or imagined. Music carries us on
Paths we cannot always pursue. Loss
Can be carefully softened in sweet
Creations and caresses from the celestial
Realms we may someday hear together.

Local Trips

When I travel now, I avoid
Flying as much as possible. Private
Jets would be an appealing way
To travel if it were not
For the expense. I mostly tour
By car. I have started seeing
All the places I once observed
With my immediate and extended family.
Local trips near my hometown hasten
A great deal of delight. People
Have often changed, only the locations
Are retained. Sometimes I remember them
As they existed as their signage
In each era's style. The feelings,
Sounds, and the images of selection
Retain the gainable hopes happiness ordains.

Gifting

The only gifts I greatly appreciate
Receiving are the ones that add
Lightness and joy to the giver.
Grace is the gift of company.
I like to give gifts too.
The more I know someone treasures
The good times and abundant moments,
The more I hope they heal
From past hurts and challenging passages
Journeyed. Gifts are often excesses created
By the resourceful who know how
Helping others to find more happiness
Usually arrives with ideas that atone.

Retired Neighbors

Someday, I hope you are lucky
Enough to live near retired neighbors
Whose words reveal sound, deep roots
And whose actions are trails along
Partitions that provide space for each
Day to be a dahlia. May
Your retired neighbors' waves reach you
Gently like soft breezes around corners.
May unhurried occasions on your path
Earn you unannounced home visits expected.
May you (like them) tend to
The harvests of invitation as life
Lightly sips the tea of tales
From the ones who are slowly
Becoming the best able to teach
How important it is to enjoy
The golden leaves of leisurely days.

Add Time

A warm beverage upon waking up
Seems to add a little time
To the new day. Carpe diem.
Coffee often measures my favorite days.
I often lack lots of time
These days to let it cool.
On the weekends, I find ways
To keep the coffee continuously flowing.
When I want to add time,
I easily remember the early mornings
I spent with my parents sharing
Coffee and creatively planning our futures.
After my morning coffee, I may
Be present and in the moment.
Now, I am in the past
With my dreams. Maybe, I'll graciously
Live the most with what remains.

Local Works

I sometimes organize books I buy
By location. Local history and memoir
Are positioned together. I like poetry
To have its own delights divided
Into two sections: place-based, local poets
And everything else. Fiction and nonfiction
Often inhabit sturdy, separate bookshelves dedicated
To what is nearby and approachable.
I have shed too many tears
Trying to get my money's worth
From reading the distant daily digests.
I treasure the flurries of local
Authors' publications as I find them
Through the local bookstores and readings.
When I read their locally-lived, infused
Personas as emotional histories through poems
With surprising and truthful lines, all
The distant biases I have collected
Through the years begin to dissipate
In the coastal air and duff-fed,
Intelligent earth. Even when I'm away,
I let my mind wander home.

Open Doors and Windows

When I think about an image
Of the happy and hopeful, I
Feel the fresh air flowing through
Open south doors and north windows.
I sometimes see spring or summer
Meandering and fragrant breezes moving fabric.
I hear music in the moutains.
I recognize the grip of gravel.
I take steps east then west.

May unhurried occassions on your path

Earn you unannounced home visits expected.

—

Notes

Mast Years: Poems uses the form: wordcount, a.k.a, (isoverbal prosody) as a "loose metrical structure" as elucidated by Lewis Turco in *"The New Book of Forms: A Handbook of Poetics"* (University Press of New England: Hanover and London, 1986).

Acknowledgments

Thank you (to my lovely wife), Sarah Craig, who is immensely talented and a key supporter of my writing journey these last few years. She is the talented author of *The Holiday Window Painting Book.* Her MBA from Western Governors University and her Bachelor of Science in Journalism from the University of Oregon, original artwork, and publishing praxis through Thoughts on the Good Life Press made it possible for this fourth collection of poems to find its way out into the world.

Thank you, Michael McGriff, for recommending the works of Lewis Turco.

A warm and heartfelt thank you to my family and friends. Thanks for keeping me company on this journey. Your feedback and support continues to inspire me. May your "Mast Years" always arrive right on time.

GUY CRAIG is from Coos Bay, Oregon, where he grew up along the South Fork Coos River. He lives in Tigard, Oregon, and he spends much of his free time in the Coos River Valley.

He holds a Master of Science in Special Education from the University of Oregon and a Bachelor of Science in Psychology from Portland State University. Guy is the author of three other poetry collections: *Coos River Reverberations: Poems of River, Farm & Forest (2021)*; *Amble (2021)*; and, *Idling Intuitions: Poems (2022)*.

Other Books by Thoughts on the Good Life Press

Coos River Reverberations:

Poems of River, Farm & Forest

By Guy Craig

Amble

By Guy Craig

Idling Intuitions: Poems

By Guy Craig

The Holiday Window Painting Book:

How to Create Colorful Holiday Magic

By Sarah Craig

www.ingramcontent.com/pod-product-compliance
Lightning Source LLC
Chambersburg PA
CBHW060411080526
44583CB00012B/527